CW01316555

Nature is a Powerhouse of Electricity! Physics Books for Kids

Children's Physics Books

BABY PROFESSOR
EDUCATION KIDS

Speedy Publishing LLC
40 E. Main St. #1156
Newark, DE 19711
www.speedypublishing.com
Copyright 2017

All Rights reserved. No part of this book may be reproduced or used in any way or form or by any means whether electronic or mechanical, this means that you cannot record or photocopy any material ideas or tips that are provided in this book.

In this book, we're going to talk about electricity in nature. So, let's get right to it!

You walked across the carpet in your house during the winter, and then you touched a doorknob. Ouch! That hurt! You just got stung by a little bit of static electricity. We've harnessed electricity to run our manmade power lines, appliances, and electric motors, but electricity exists on and around Earth in lots of natural forms.

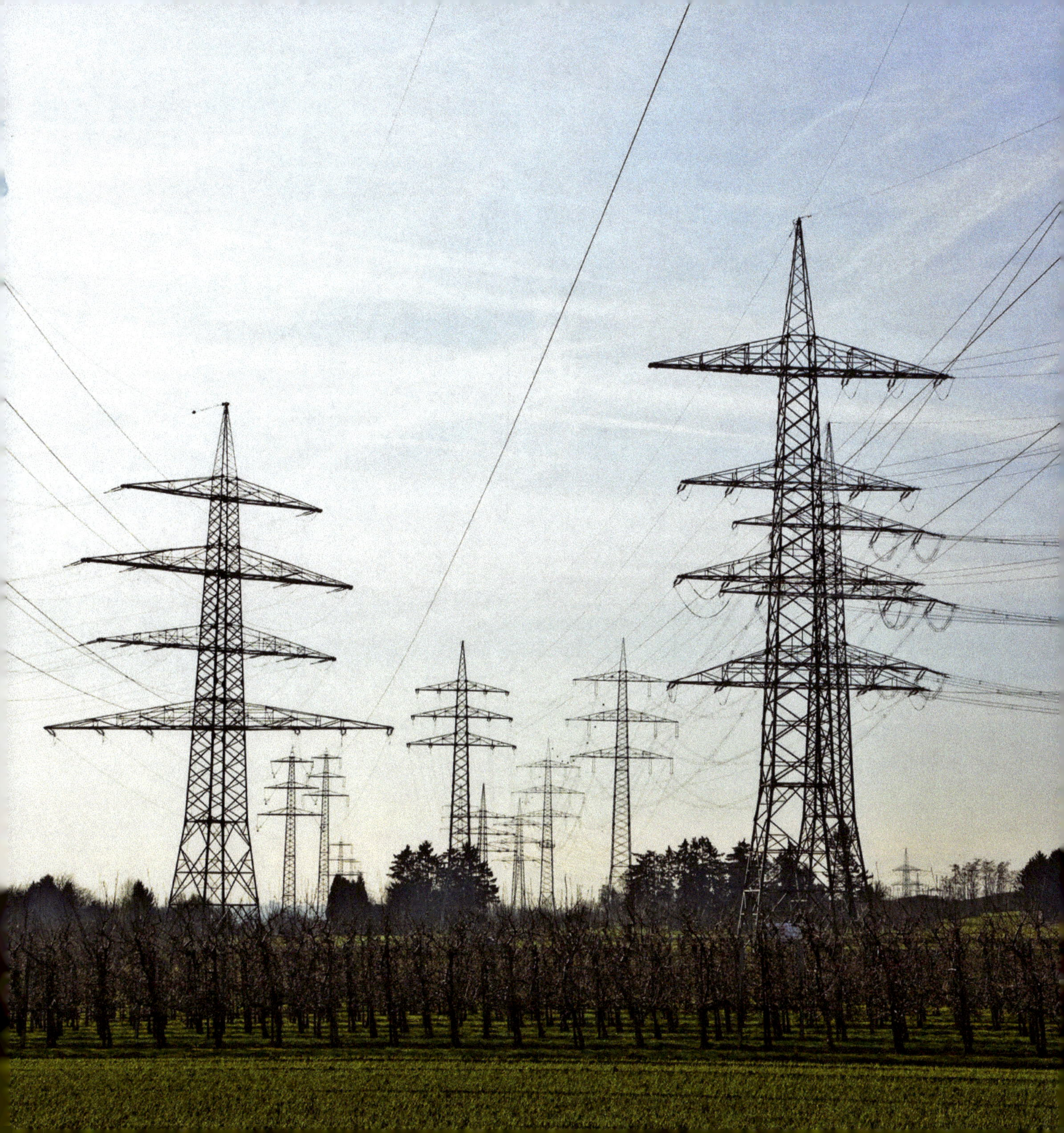

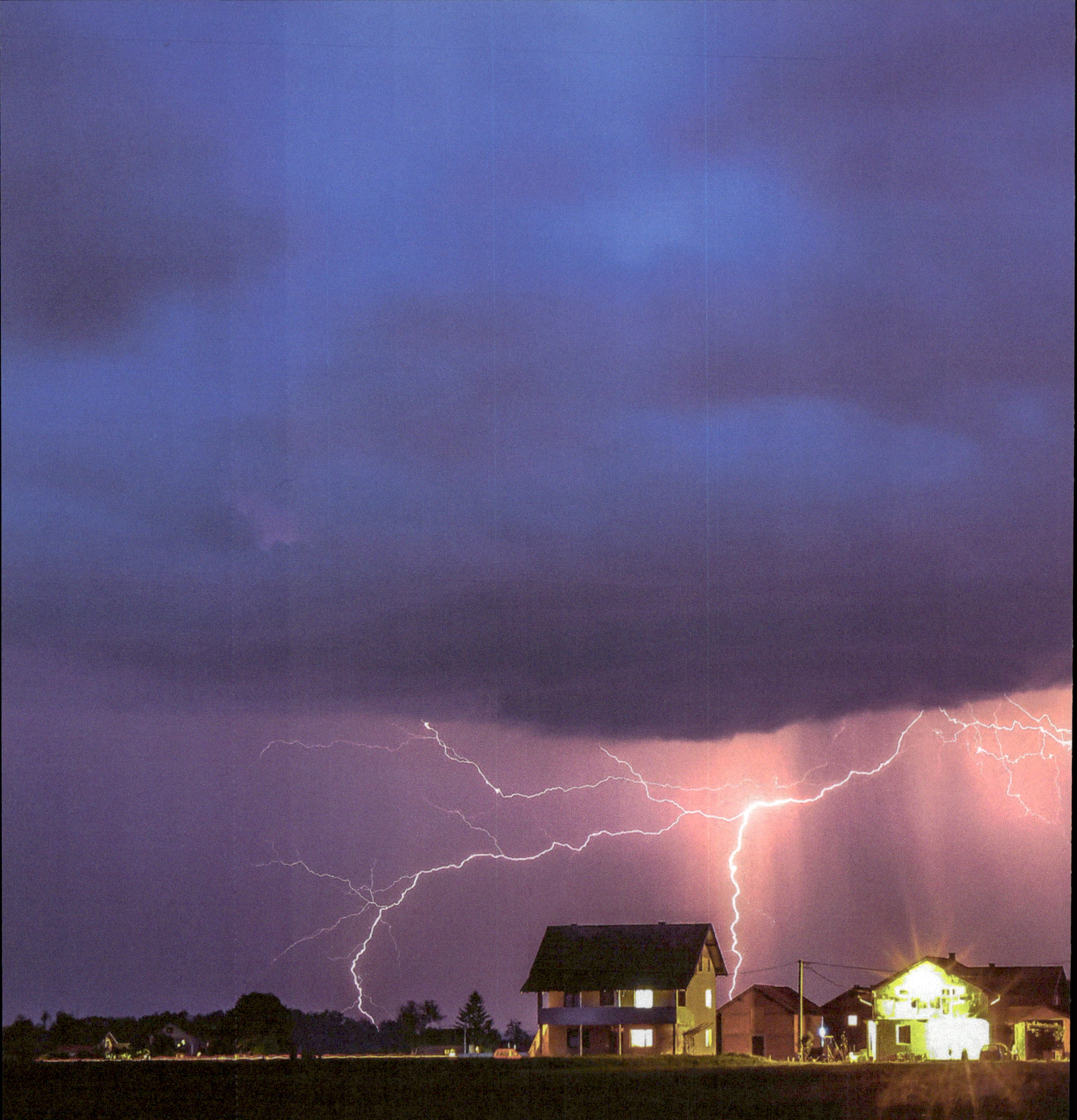

There's nowhere you could go to hide from electricity. It's inside your body, inside the bodies of other animals, and you can see powerful displays of it every time there's a thunderstorm.

LIGHTNING

Perhaps the most dramatic display of natural electricity is lightning. Lightning is basically a very powerful current of electricity. As thunderclouds form in the atmosphere, small particles of ice that are like frozen raindrops start bumping into each other as they're moving in the air. All this activity creates a charge of electricity. After a period of time, the entire cloud or group of clouds is filled with charges of electricity.

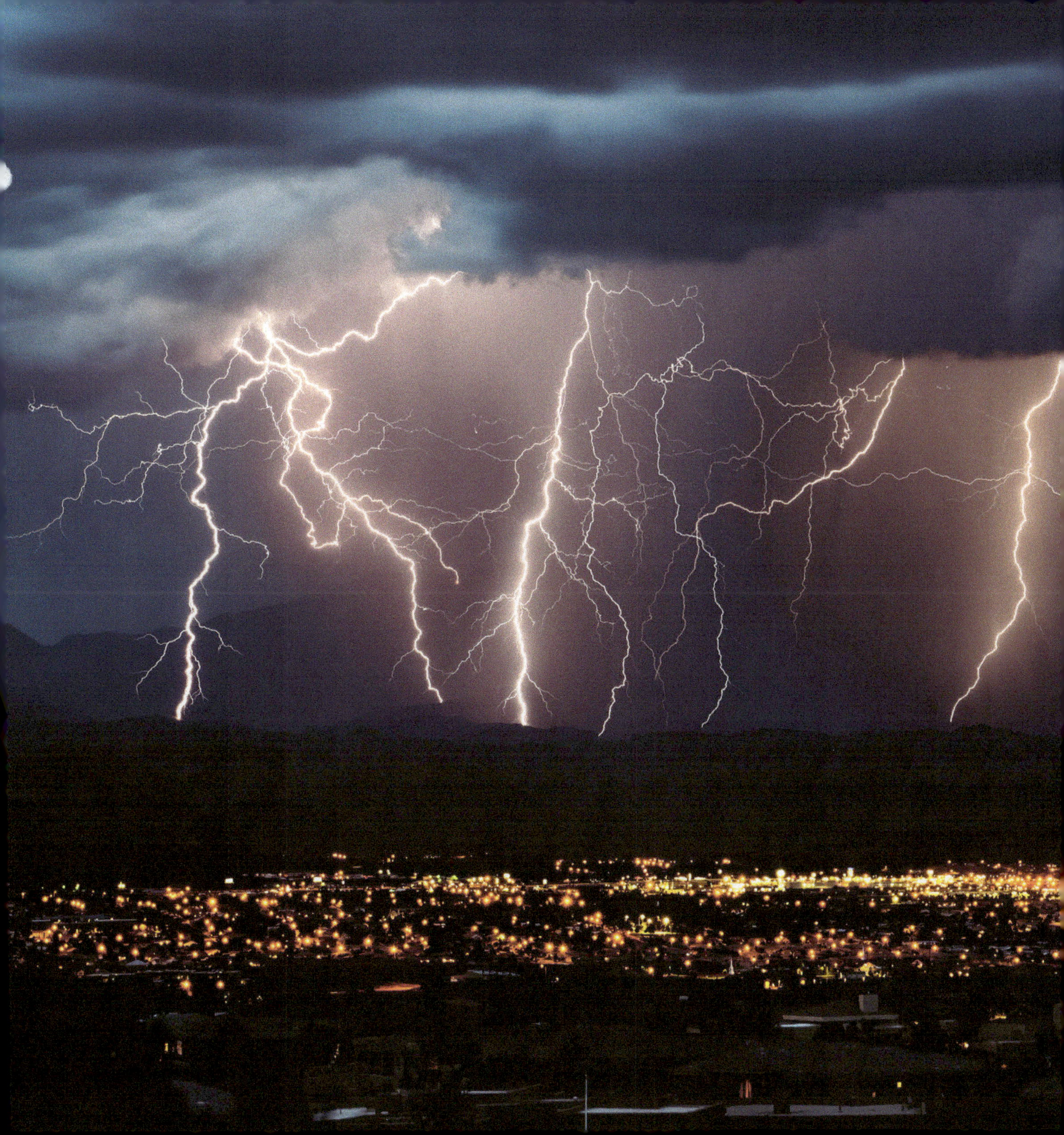

This is happening at the atomic level and the positive charges, which are protons, gather at the top of the thundercloud. The negative charges gather in the bottom portion of the cloud. Since these opposite charges attract each other, a positive charge also starts to build up on the area of ground beneath where the cloud is positioned.

The electrical charge from the ground starts to concentrate on anything that's sticking up from the ground both natural and manmade, such as mountains, tall buildings, animals, or people.

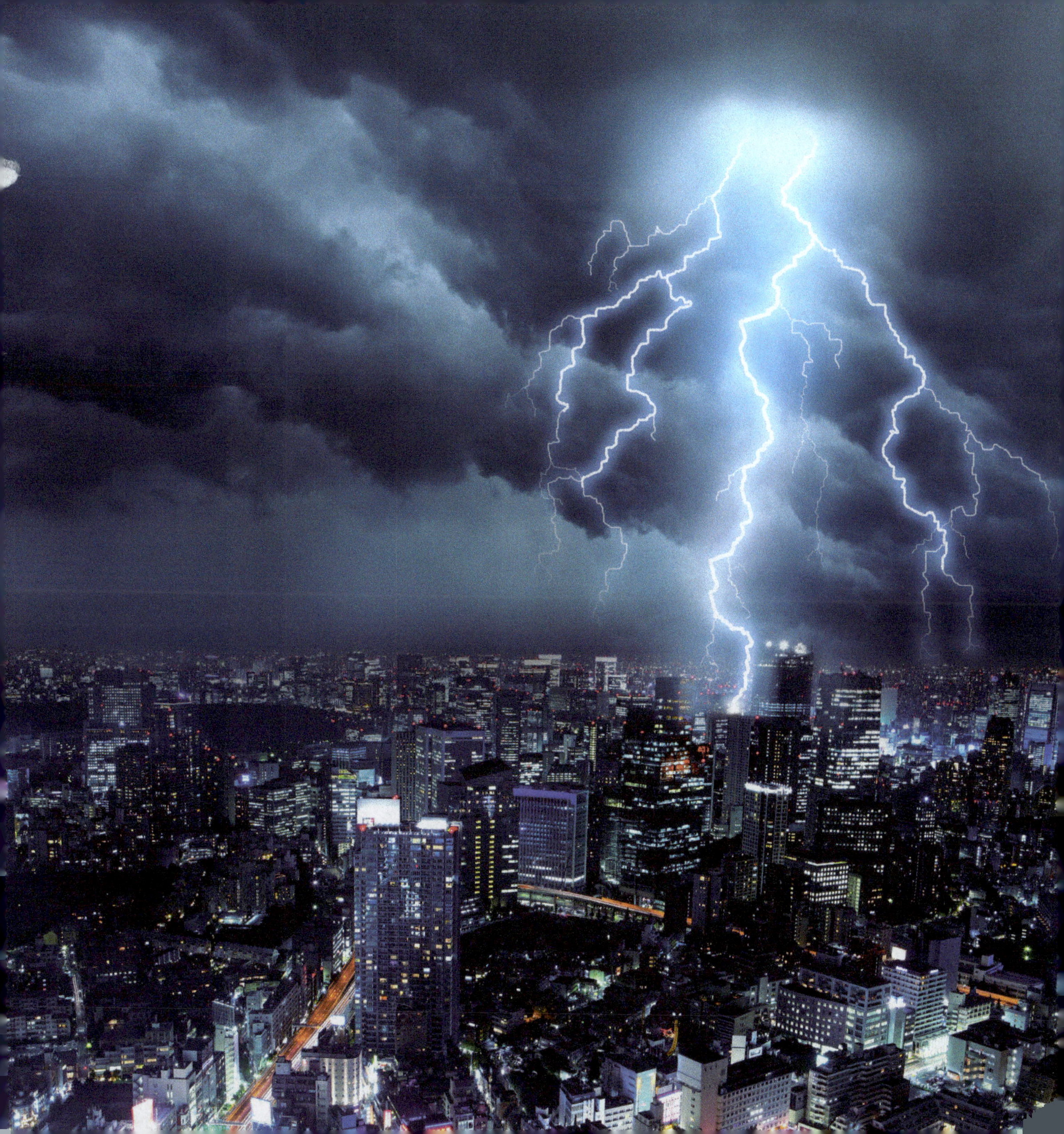

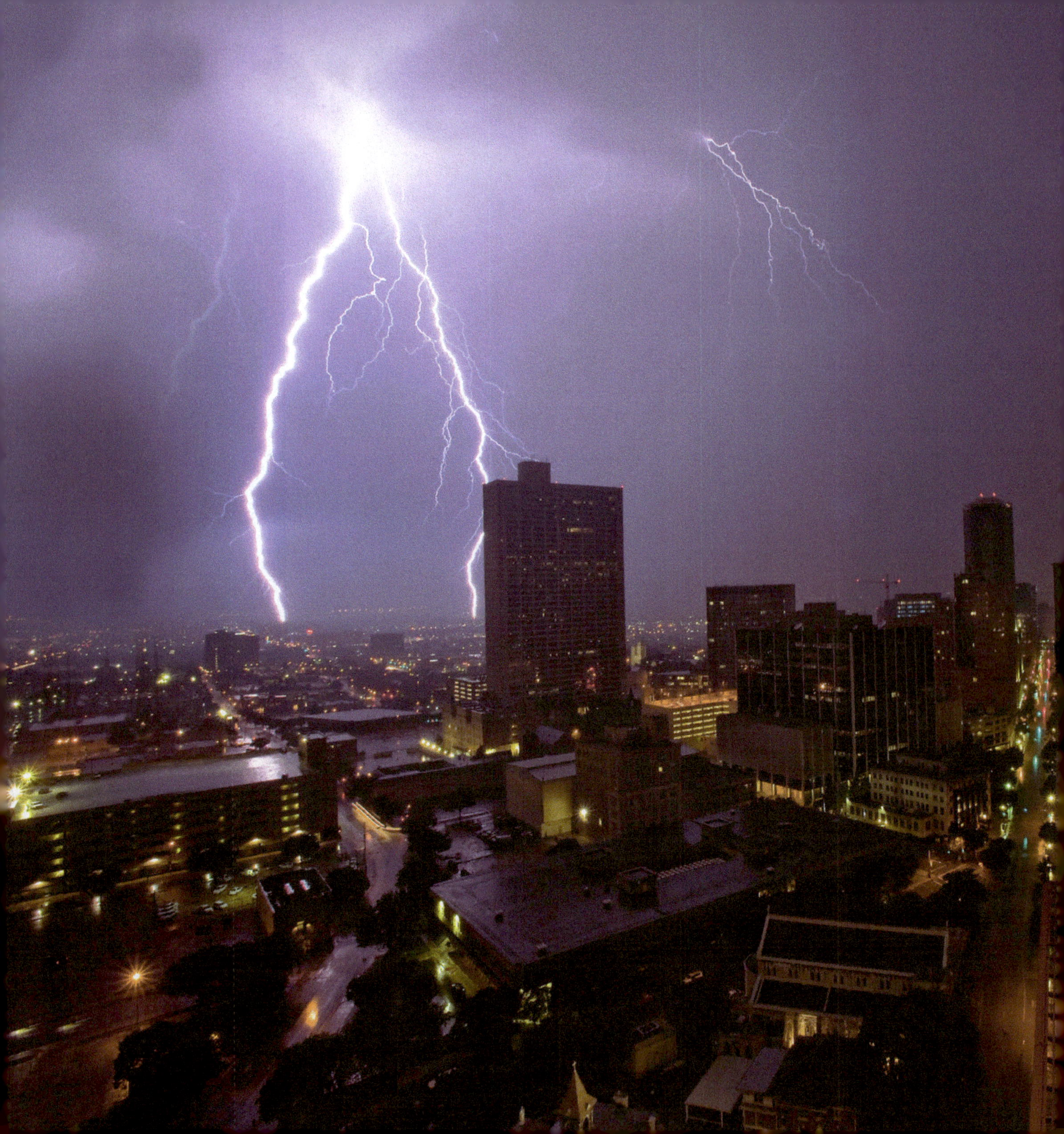

Eventually, the charge from these ground locations connects with a charge that's extending from the clouds and then a powerful bolt of lightning strikes. This is why thunderstorms are very dangerous.

There are over 3 million flashes of lightning every day around the world. That's about 40 flashes of lightning every second! Lightning flashes can happen within the same cloud, between two clouds, and between the thunderclouds and the ground. In the United States, about 100 people are killed every year by lightning and hundreds more are injured. It's never safe to be outdoors during thunderstorms.

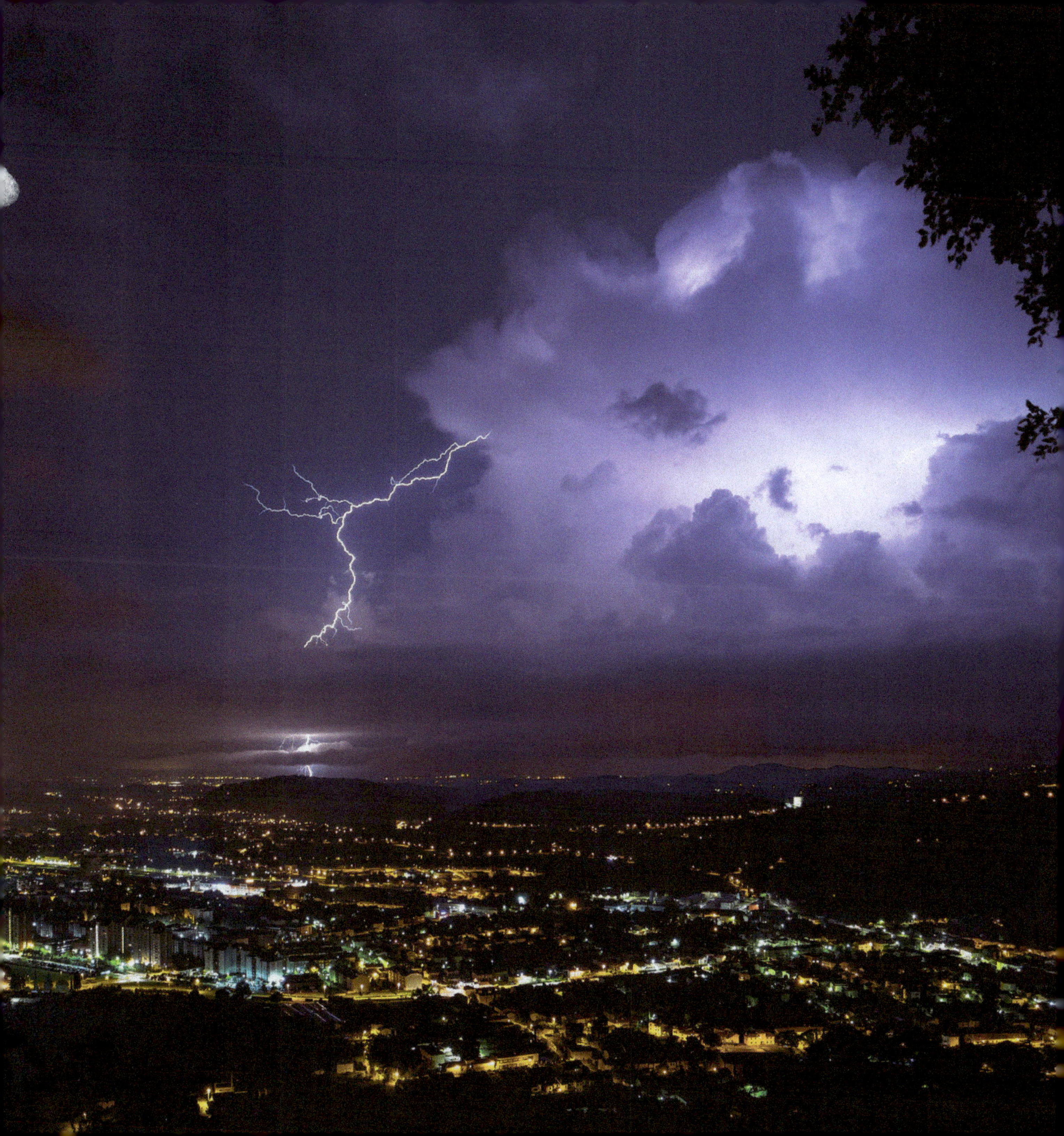

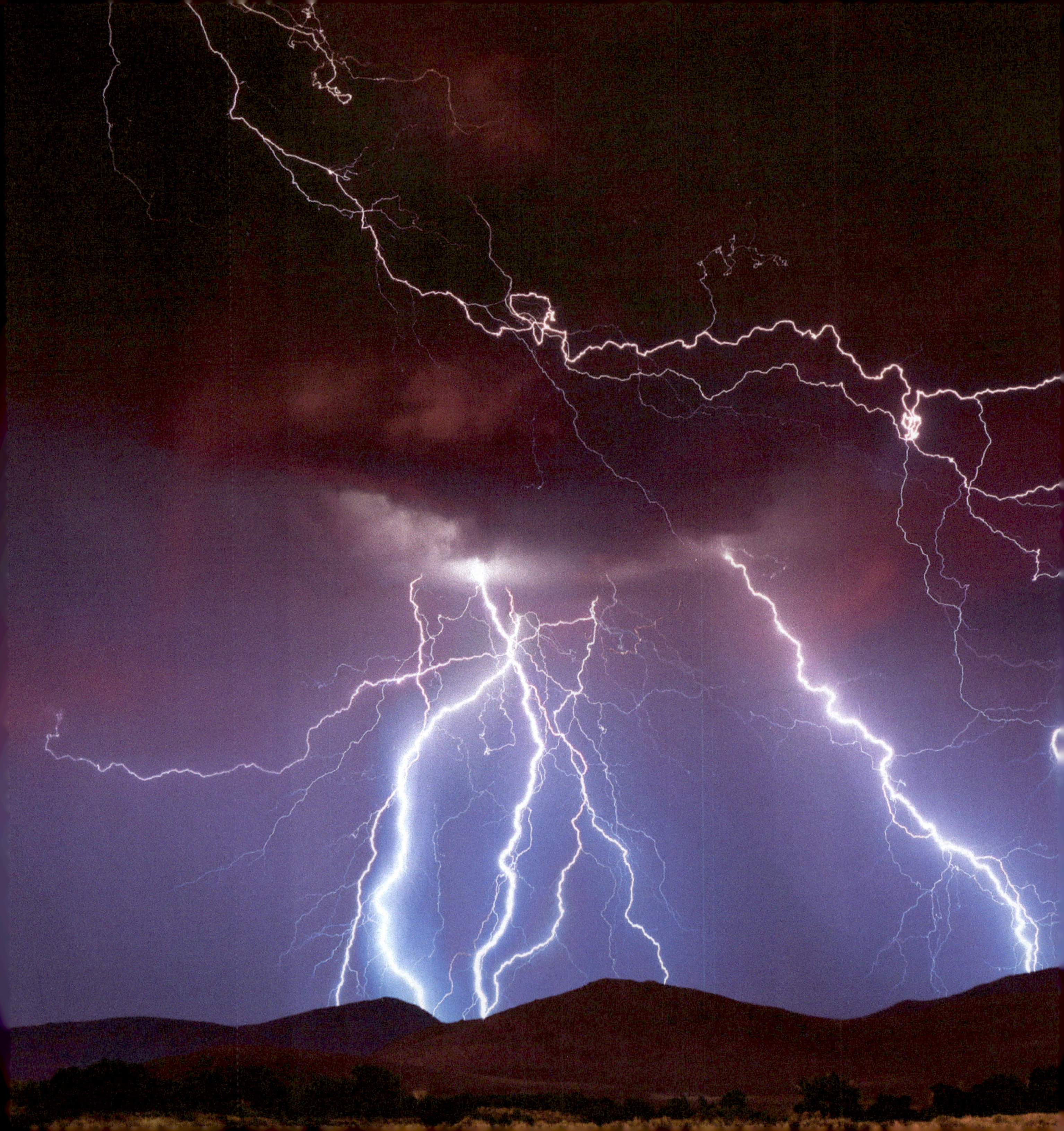

Catatumbo Lightning

Bubbles of methane gas frozen into clear ice

There's methane in the swamps, which is highly flammable. This gas combined with the winds from the Andes Mountains makes the atmosphere there very volatile.

This is a special type of lightning that forms an arc in the sky as it goes from cloud to cloud. It's an almost permanent storm that happens in the marshlands.

There's actually a place on Earth where lightning strikes almost every night and strikes 20,000 times in a 10-hour span of time. It's called Catatumbo lightning. This happens at the entrance to the Catatumbo River that is fed by Lake Maracaibo in the country of Venezuela.

Urban Lightning Storm

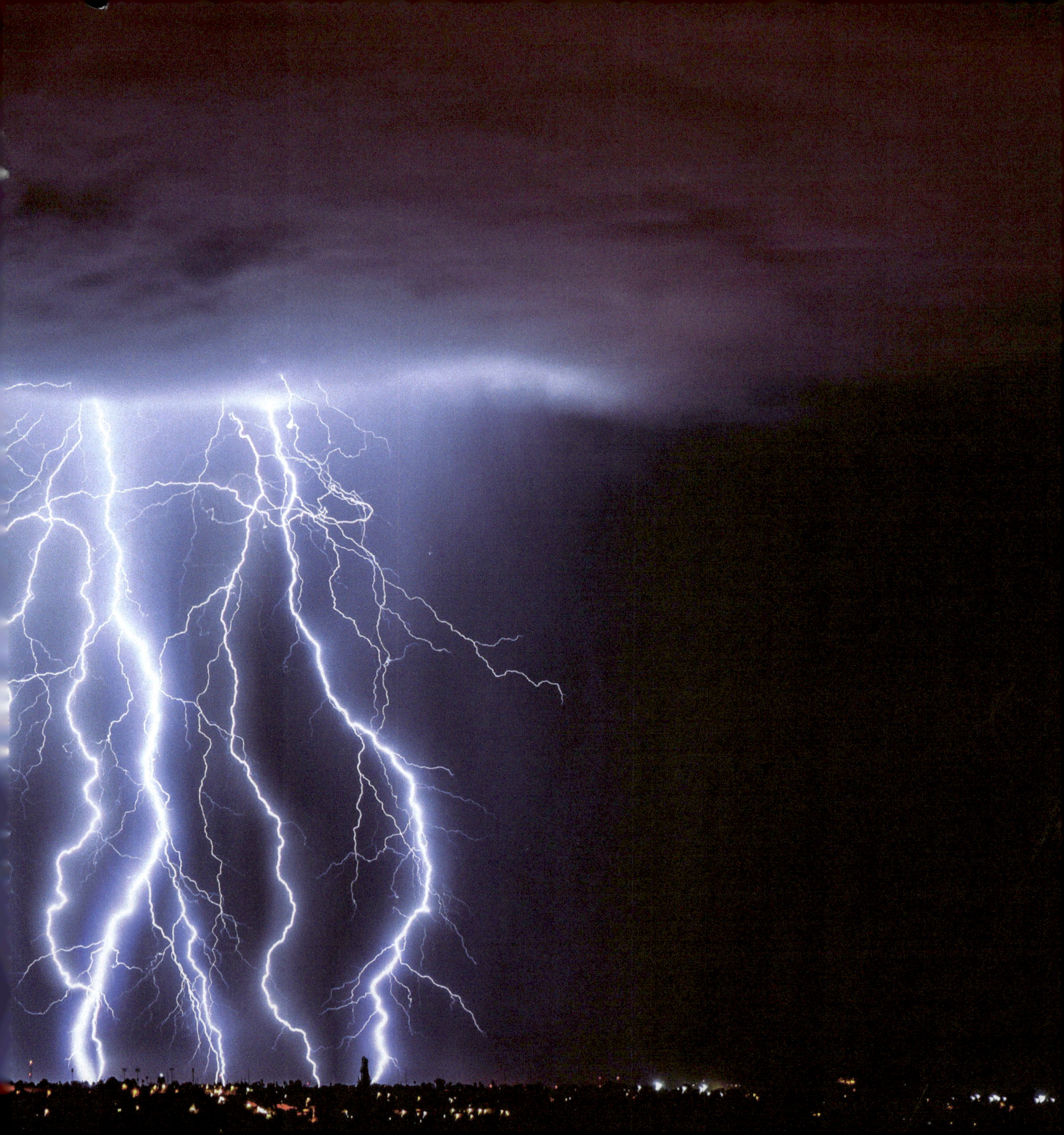

The air inside lightning gets so heated up that it changes into plasma. When the gas transforms into plasma, the expansion creates a thunderous shockwave that we can hear. Because light travels so fast and sound travels much more slowly, the sound from thunder happens well after the lightning has struck.

Even though a flash of lightning is only one inch wide, its temperature is 15,000 degrees Fahrenheit to as hot as 60,000 degrees Fahrenheit. By comparison, the surface of the sun is 9,000 degrees Fahrenheit. A single flash of lightning can carry an electrical current as powerful as 300,000 amperes. The electrical wiring in your house carries about 20 to 30 amperes.

The lightning discharges at Catatumbo are so frequent that they help to replenish the ozone in our atmosphere. The mysterious Catatumbo lightning has an orange-red color and can seen for hundreds of miles away acting as a natural lighthouse.

In 2010, the lightning stopped for two months. The last time this had happened in recorded history was in 1906. The natives who live in the area were relieved when the lightning returned.

Catatumbo Lightning

A tiger looking for food

ELECTRICITY IN ANIMALS

Just like human beings, other animals have electricity within their bodies. Electrical impulses send signals from their brains to their body parts so they can move. In addition to these normal functions, some animals use electricity to sense their environment, to thwart predators that might eat them, and to find food.

One animal that uses a lot of electricity is the electric eel. This ocean creature, which is actually related to the catfish and isn't a true eel, has an amazing ability. It has two special organs inside its abdomen that take up about 80% of the internal structure of its body. It uses its power to stun prey in the water so that it can eat them. It can emit up to 650 volts of electricity, which is enough to kill a large mammal.

Electric Eel

Spiracle

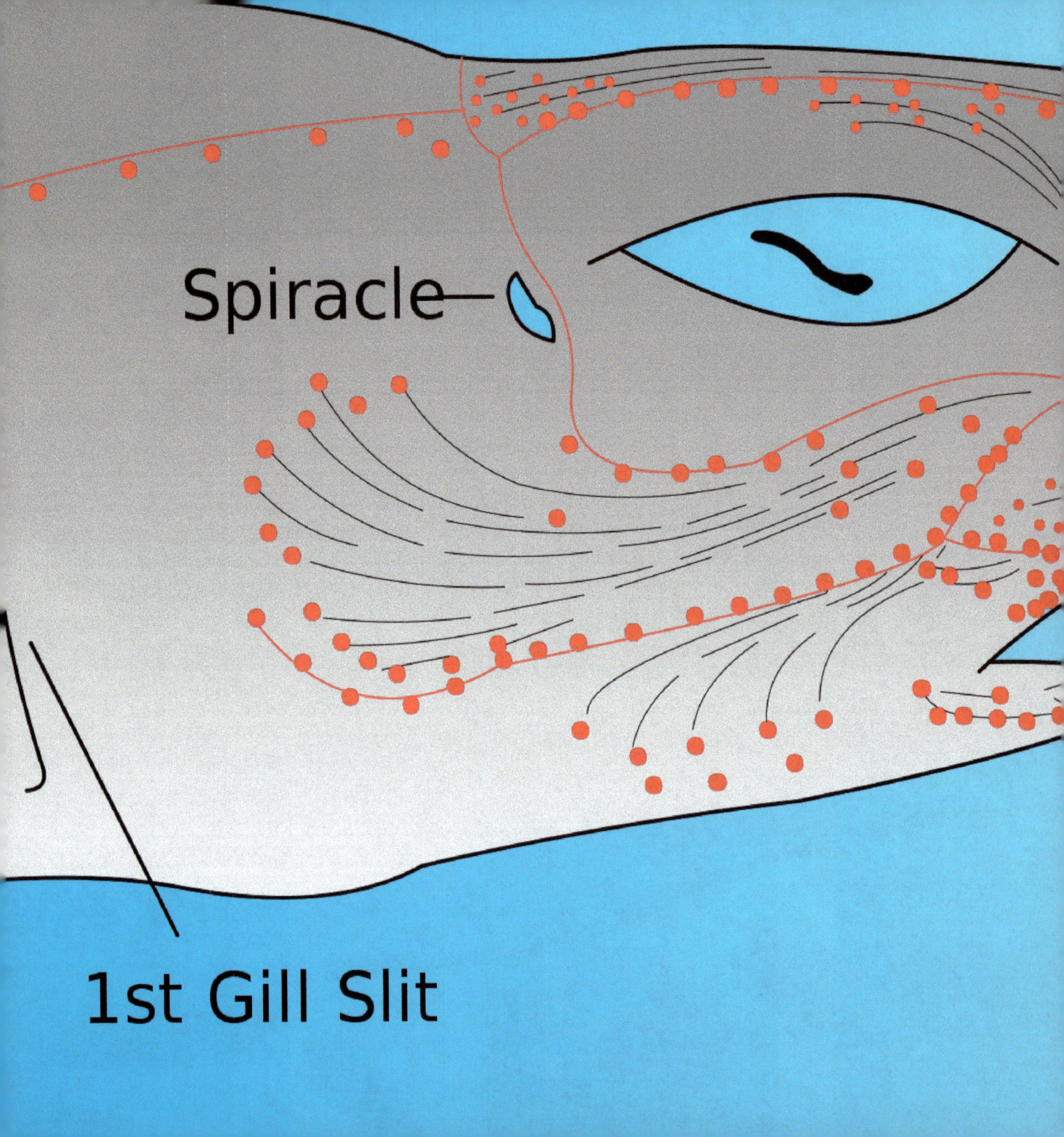

1st Gill Slit

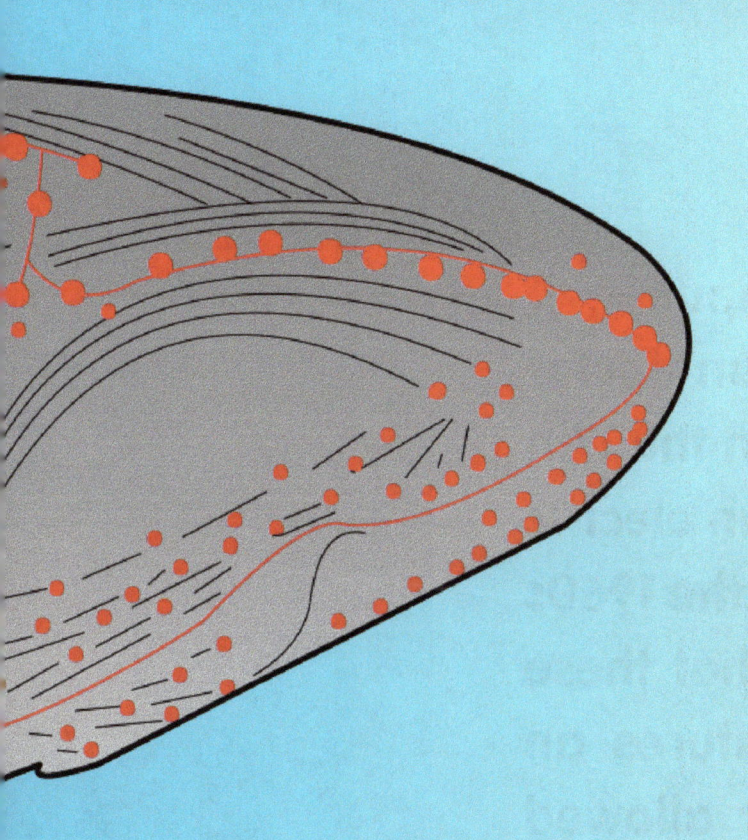

Another interesting example of the use of electricity by animals in the water is called **electroreception**. Sharks as well as rays, sawfish, and skates can detect the electric signals given off by other creatures. They have tiny organs that are specialized just for this activity.

The organs are called **Ampullae of Lorenzini** after the Italian doctor who first discovered them in the 17th century when he dissected an electric ray. However, it wasn't until the 1960s that scientists discovered that these organs gave the sea creatures an entirely different sense. It allowed them to pick up the electrical signals from other animals even if they were buried deep under the ocean floor. It's a sense that helps them hunt prey.

Lorenzini

Human Brain

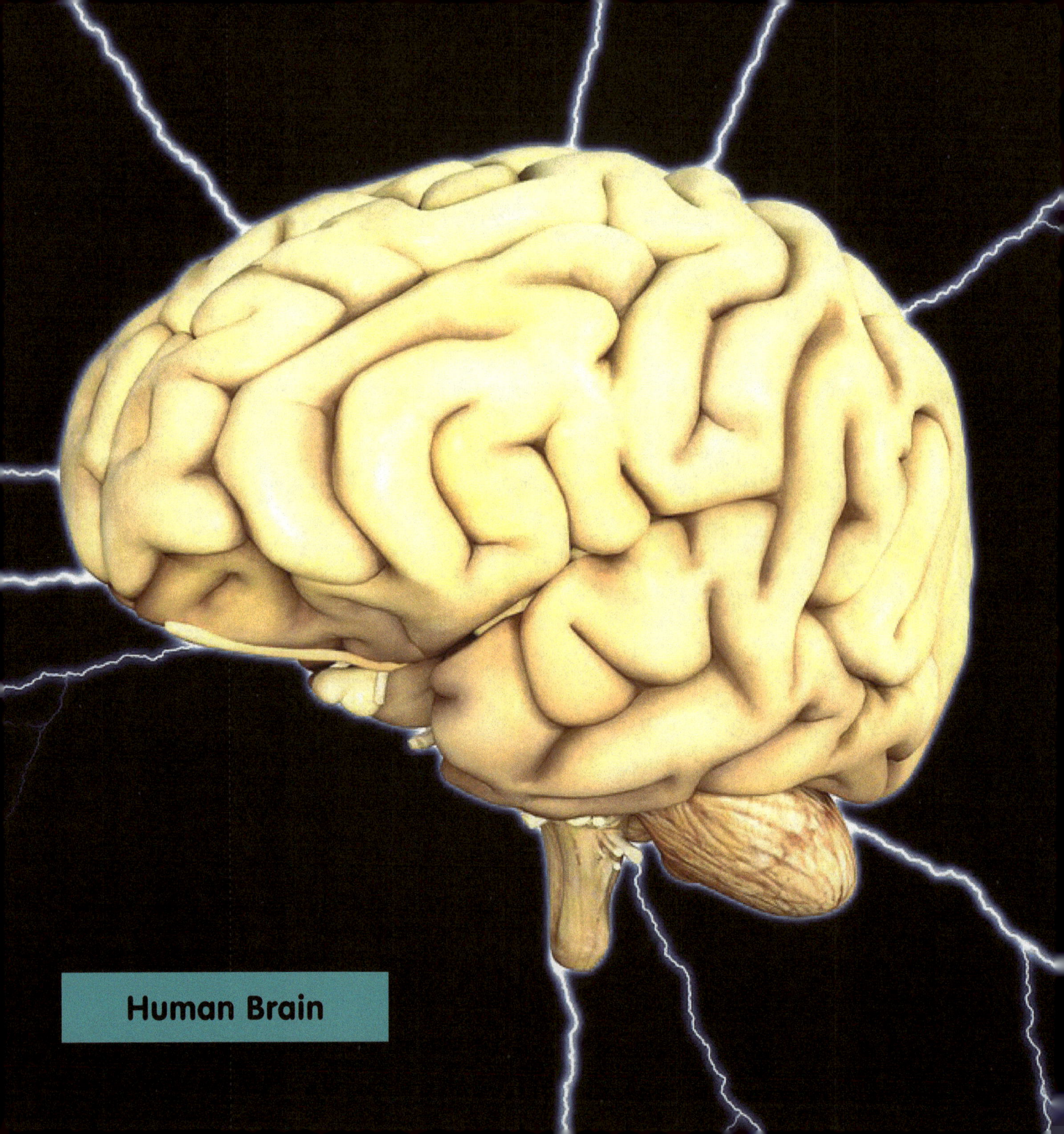

ELECTRICITY IN THE HUMAN BODY

Human beings and most animals have complex nervous systems throughout their bodies. In order for our muscles to move, our brains must tell them to do so. This is done by the brain sending an electrical signal that travels down the nerves to stimulate the muscles into action. The electricity is generated by chemical reactions from the different molecules of our bodies.

STATIC ELECTRICITY

Another form of electricity in nature is static electricity. You've probably experienced static electricity quite a few times. Maybe you walked across the carpet and shuffled your feet. When you touched your dog or a door handle, you got a small shock. Maybe you took off a knit cap and all your hair was standing on end or you rubbed a balloon on your clothes and made it stick on the wall. All these are examples of static electricity.

Static Electricity

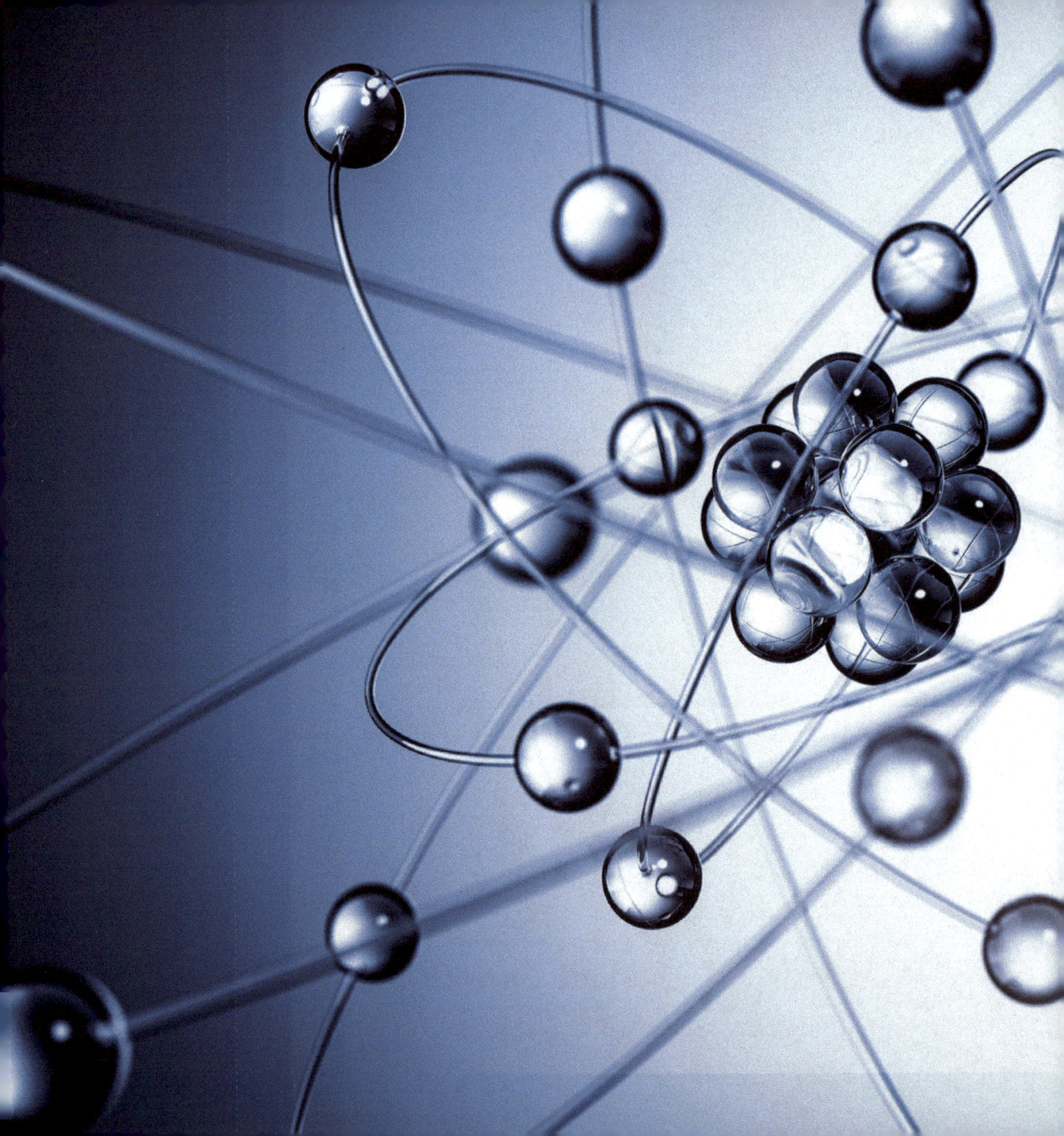

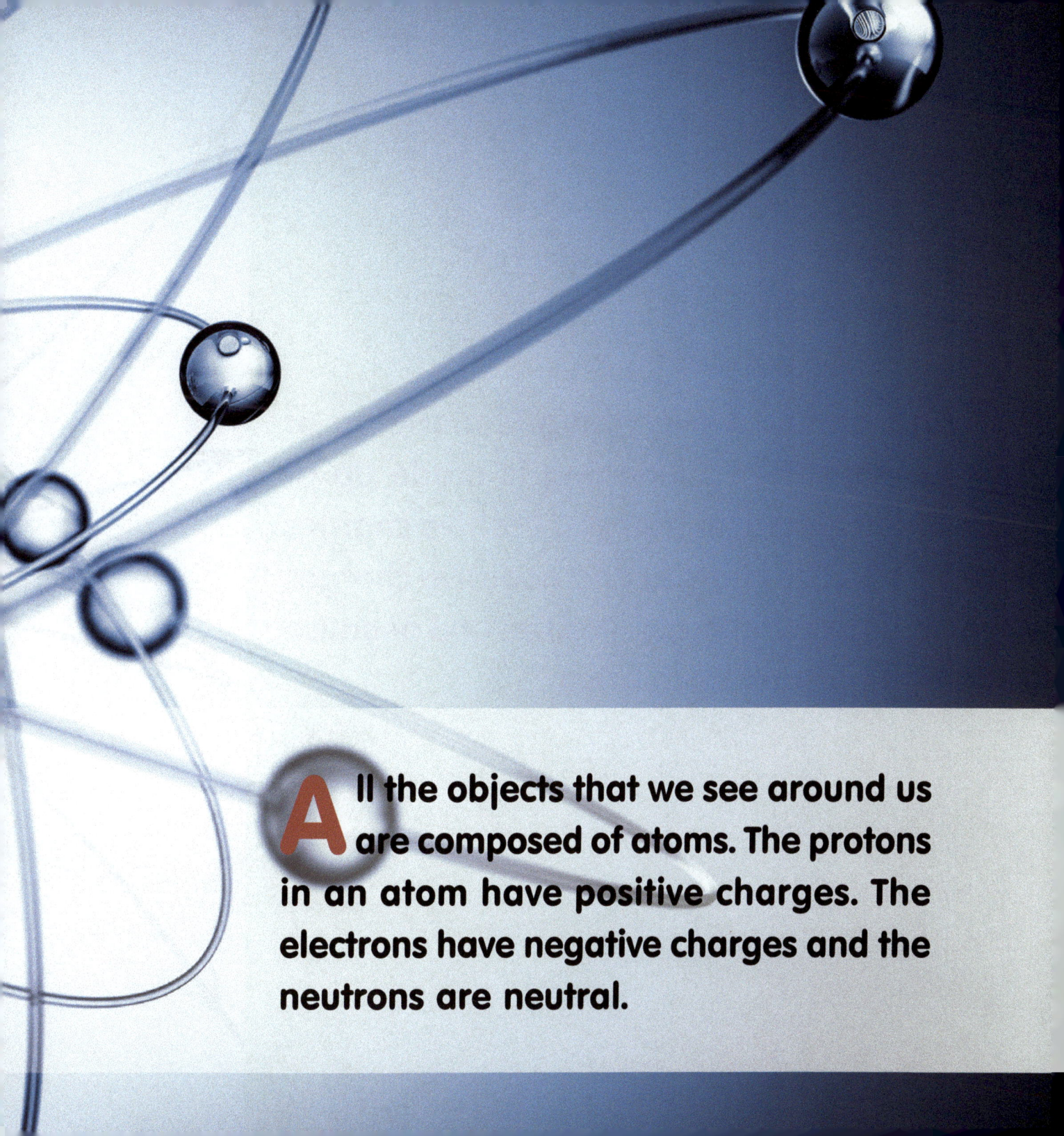

All the objects that we see around us are composed of atoms. The protons in an atom have positive charges. The electrons have negative charges and the neutrons are neutral.

This means if everything is made up of atoms, then everything is made up of different electrical charges. Positive charges repel positive charges and negative charges repel negative charges. Positive and negative charges attract each other.

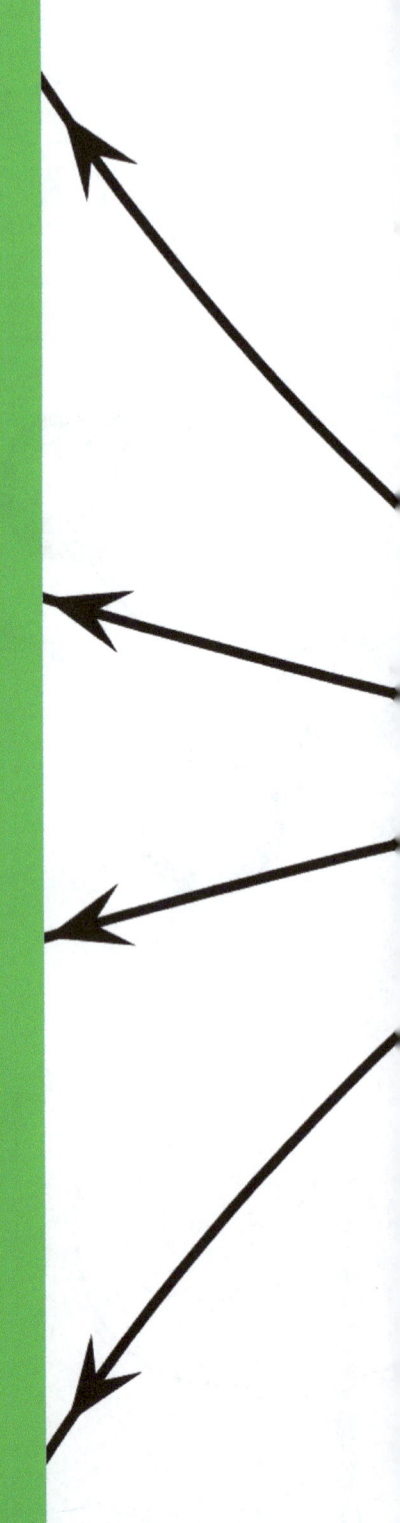

Electric Charges

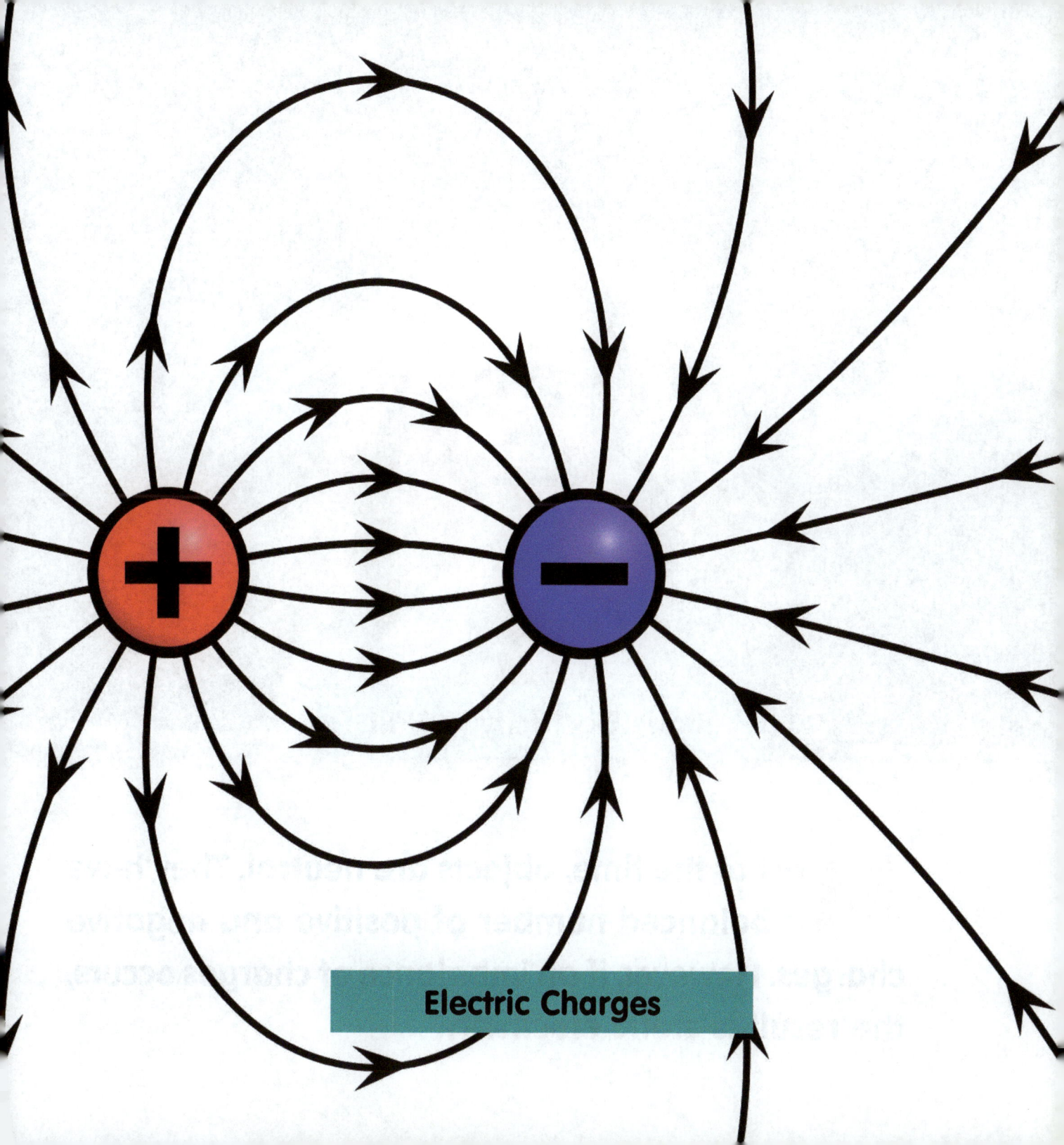

Static Electricity in Hair

Most of the time, objects are neutral. They have a balanced number of positive and negative charges. However, if an imbalance of charges occurs, the result is **static electricity**.

The charges build up on an object's surface until they can be discharged.

For example, if you shuffle your feet as you walk across a dry, thick carpet, your body collects a bunch of excess electrons. They stay on your body until you transfer them by touching your furry pet. Your extra electrons are released from your fingers to your pet, causing a quick shock and sometimes an electrical spark that flashes for a split second. It's static electricity in action!

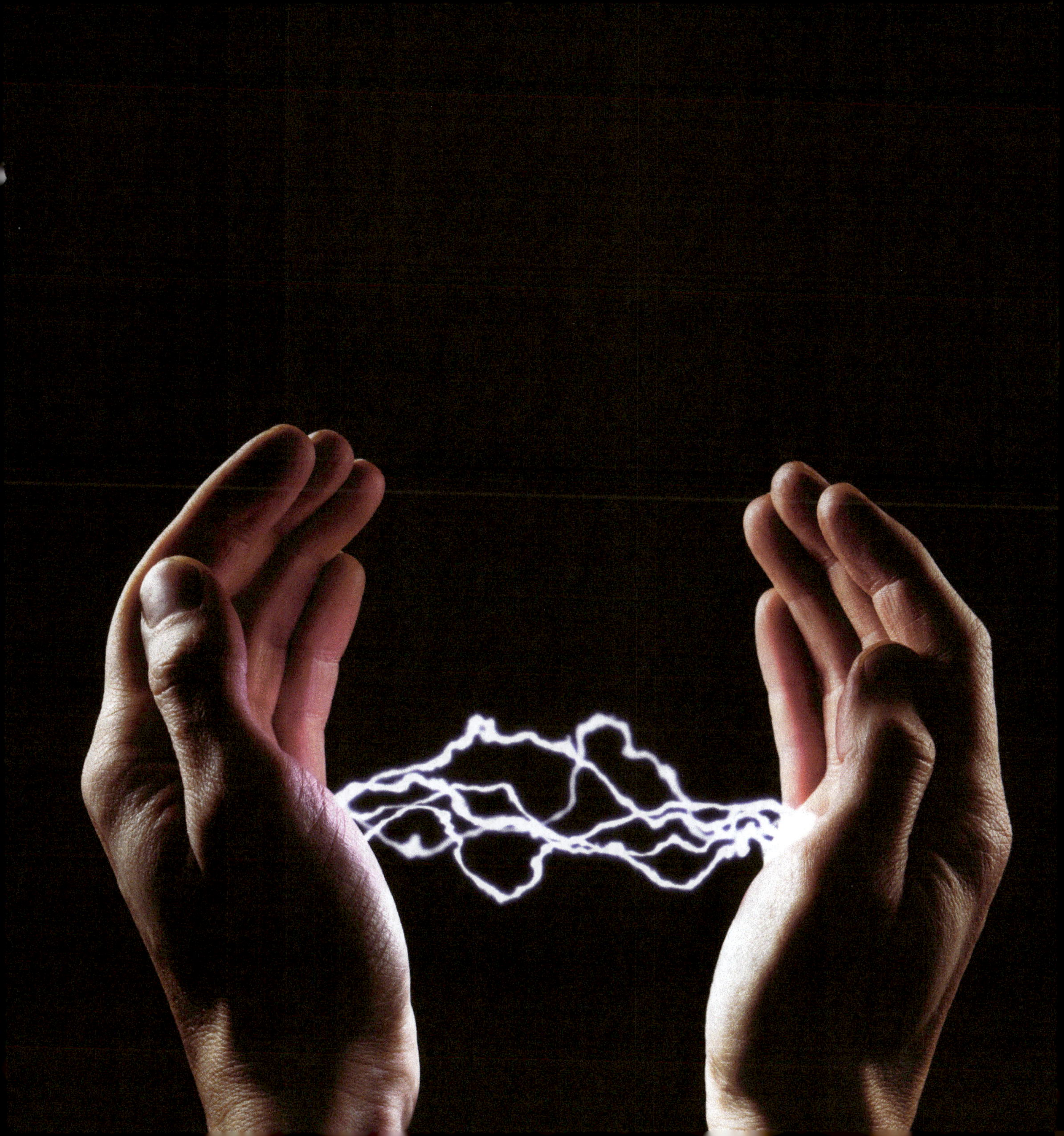

When you remove your hat, the friction causes electrons to move from the hat to your hair. Because the electrons all have the same negative charge, your hair stands on end as each strand of hair tries to get away from all the others.

Negative

Rubbing a balloon causes it to pick up negative charges. Because the wall has more positive charges than the balloon, the two opposite types of charges attract each other and the balloon sticks to the wall.

THE EARTH'S MAGNETIC CORE

The inner core of the Earth is made of iron that is solid. The outer core that surrounds the inner core is composed primarily of the element of iron and the element of nickel. These elements are very hot and they exist in liquid form.

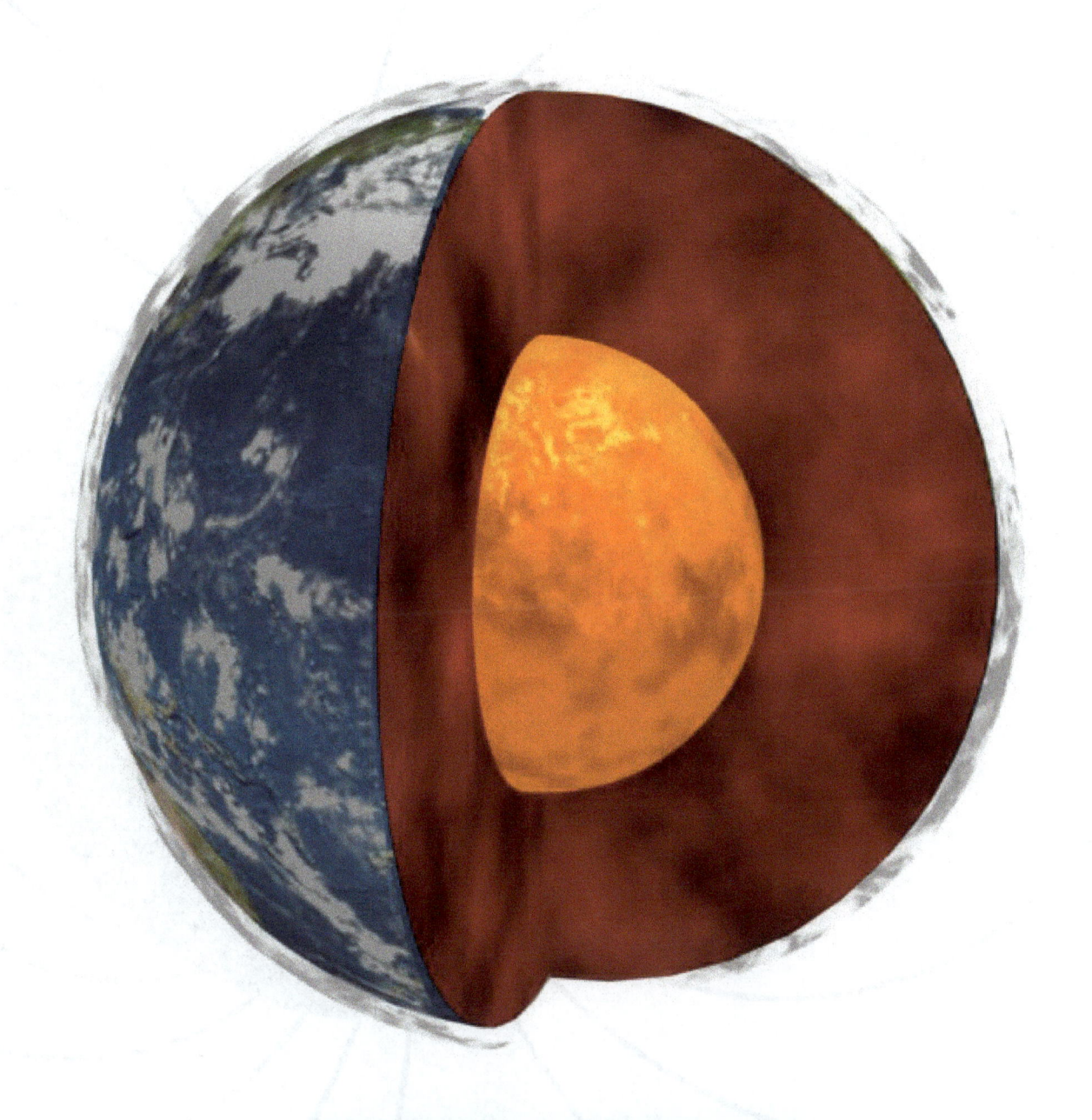

Earth's Magnetic Core

Electrical Current

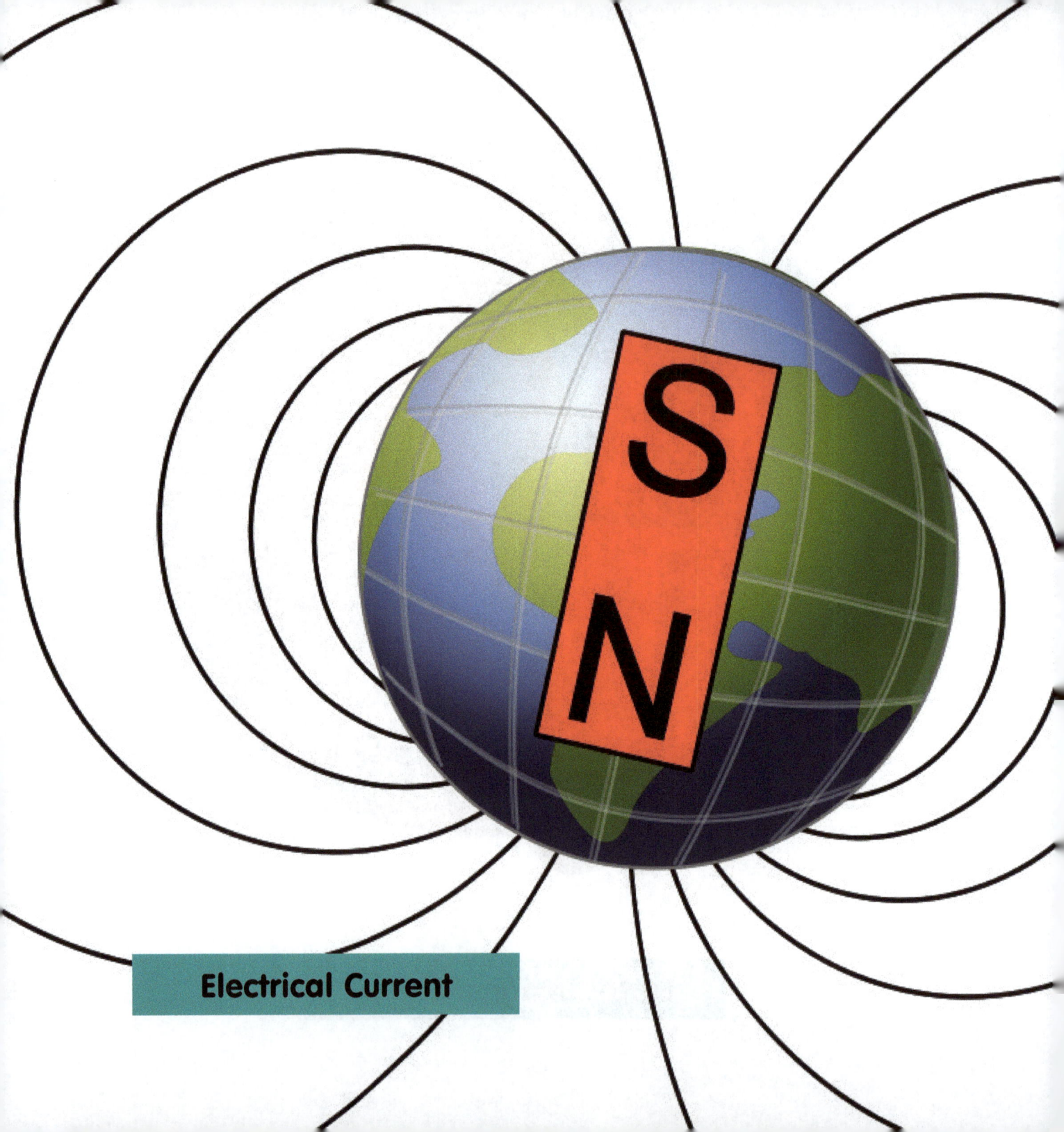

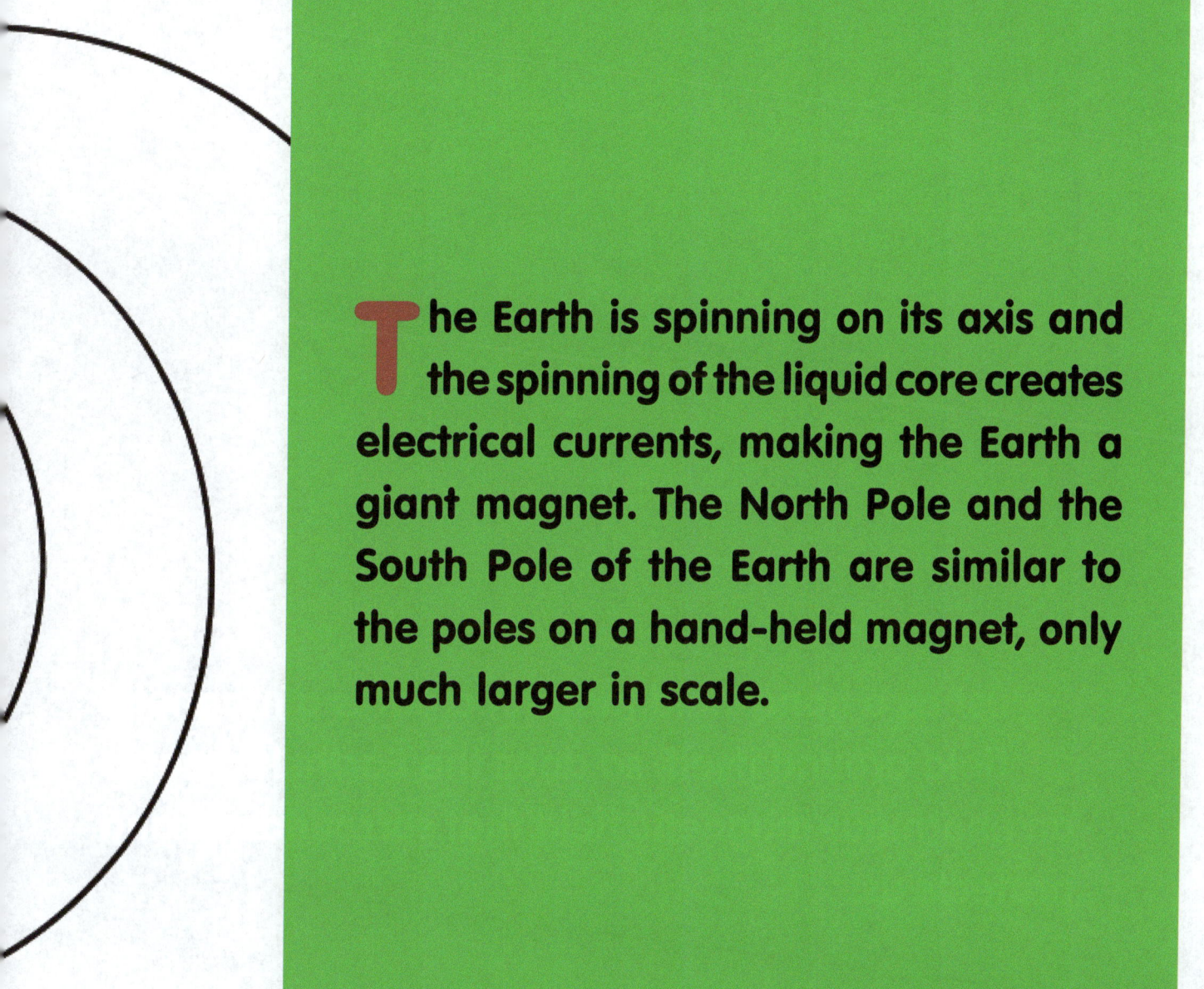

The Earth is spinning on its axis and the spinning of the liquid core creates electrical currents, making the Earth a giant magnet. The North Pole and the South Pole of the Earth are similar to the poles on a hand-held magnet, only much larger in scale.

Just as a hand-held magnet creates a magnetic field around itself, so does the Earth. It creates an enormous magnetic field that surrounds us and protects us.

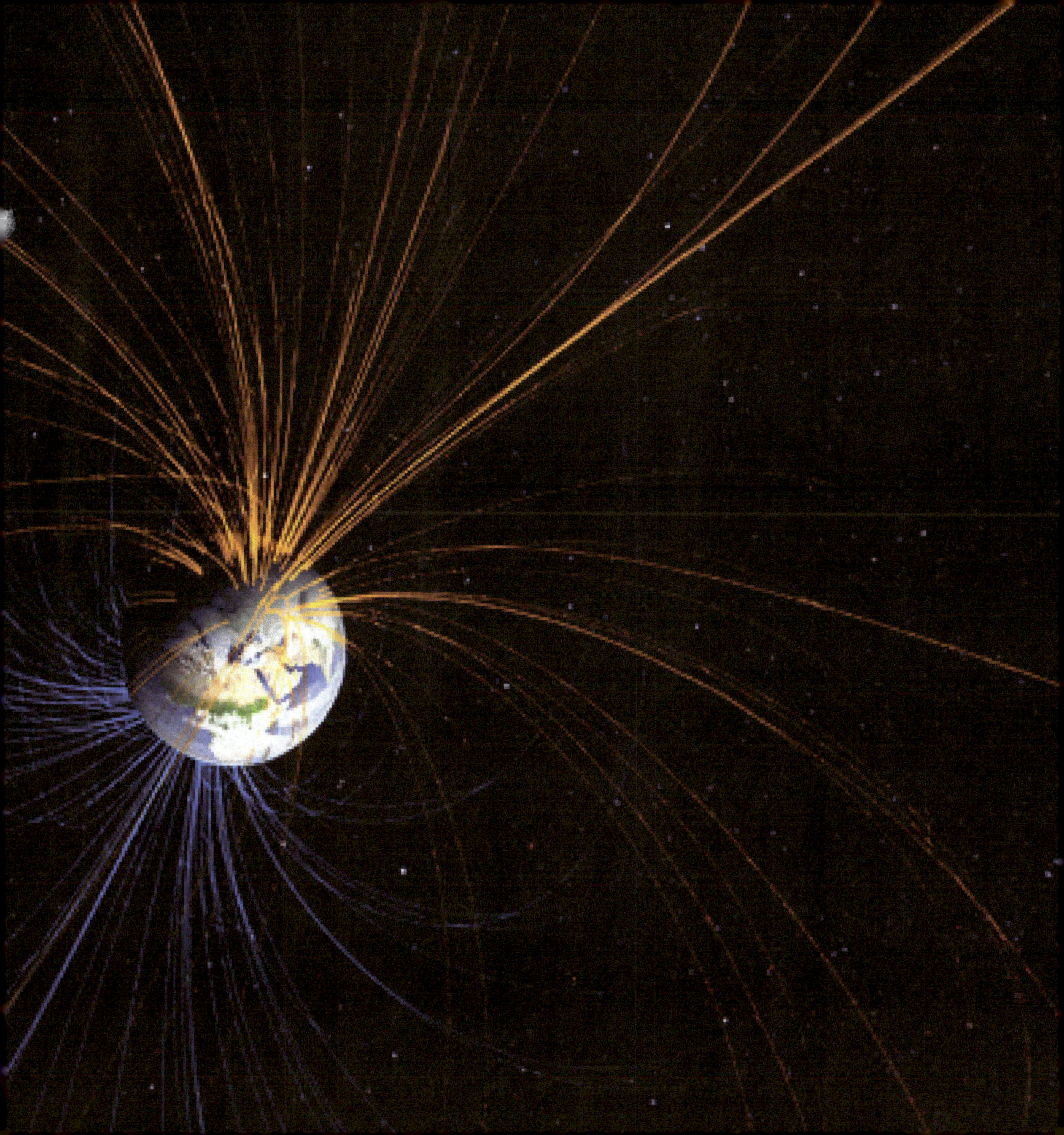

This field extends far beyond the Earth's surface. Without it, there would be no life on our planet. The reason is that it shields us from the wind from our Sun, called solar wind.

Our magnetic field is useful in other ways too. We can use a compass to tell north from south because of the magnetic field.

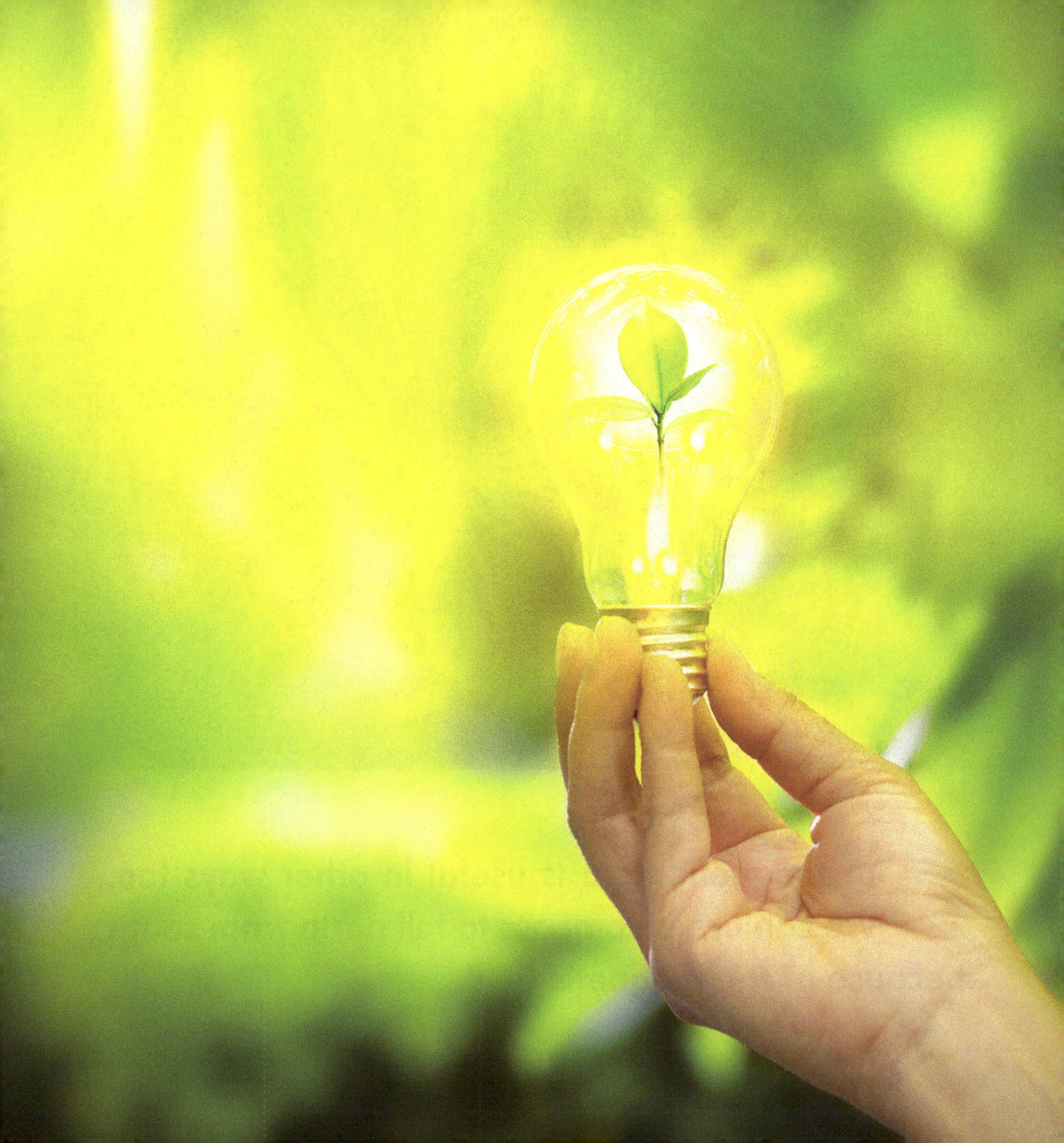

Awesome! Now you know more about the forms of electricity in nature. You can find more Physics books from Baby Professor by searching the website of your favorite book retailer.

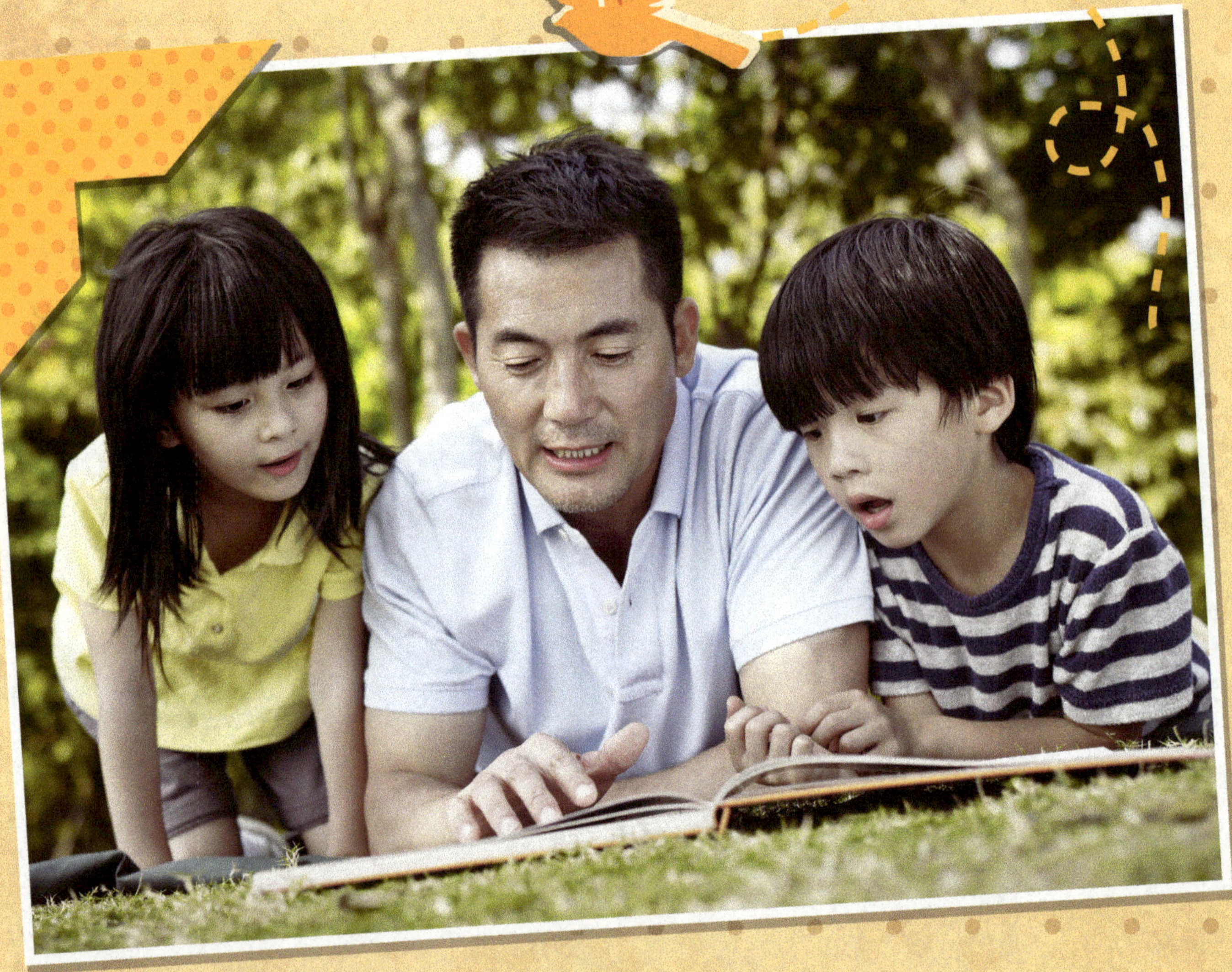

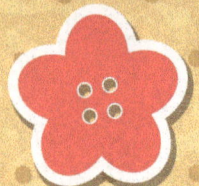

Visit

BABY PROFESSOR
EDUCATION KIDS

www.BabyProfessorBooks.com

to download Free Baby Professor eBooks and view our catalog of new and exciting Children's Books

Milton Keynes UK
Ingram Content Group UK Ltd.
UKHW051135030924
447802UK00003B/206

9 798869 412133